Contents

Fact and Fiction

About Skateboarding	2
Pride Comes Before a Fall	6
Welcome to Alton Towers	8
Alton Towers information	10

Non-chronological Reports

About Elephants	12
Key Facts about Hippos	14
Mighty Mammals	16
Snake spidergram	18
Crocodiles	20

Instructions

How to Make a Twizzer	22
How to Make a Balancing Bird	24
How to Play Tiddly-winks	26

Making Notes

The Romans	28
Roman Sports and Games	30
Gladiators	32
Children in Roman Times	34

Writing Letters

Recount	36
Complaint	37
Explanation	38
Congratulation	39
Uplands Farm Brochure	40
Kinds of Letters	42

Alphabetical Texts

Hobbies	44
Sea Fishing	46
Seamount Junior Fishing Club	47
Index	48

ABOUT SKATEBOARDING

Skateboarding started in the late 1950s on the West Coast of America. A group of bored young surfers tried to put a surfboard on rollerskate wheels!

The earliest skateboards were very dangerous. One problem was the steel wheels, which made the skateboard judder. Nowadays, skateboard wheels are made of plastic and run more smoothly.

Skating Essentials

The Board

Beginners are advised to go for a basic board. Although the ride will be less smooth and flowing, it's the easiest and cheapest way to find out if skateboarding suits you.

If you want to take it further, you will need a set-up of professional standard. (It's called a 'set-up' because you don't buy a board as such – you choose the components and the board is assembled at the shop.)

The Clothes

The local skateboard shop will sell the right clothes and safety gear. Skaters wear a proper helmet, and guards on their knees, elbows and wrists to protect against falls. It makes sense to wear heavy clothing like jeans and a long-sleeved top: you can move more easily in loose, baggy clothes.

Street or Ramp?

The two main types of skateboarding are Street and Ramp. Street skateboarding is done around town, using obstacles like kerbs, steps and handrails. This can be dangerous and is banned in some cities. However, there are skateparks which copy the urban landscape and offer a safe place to practise. Skateparks are also the place to do ramp skating. Ramps (also known as 'halfpipes') are skateable surfaces in the shape of a huge letter 'U'.

Tail
The upturned back of the skateboard is called the 'kicktail'.

Nose
The front of the skateboard is known as the nose and is slightly upturned.

Truck
Each truck is made up of two parts, the 'baseplate' which is bolted to the board and the 'hanger' which carries the wheels.

Wheel
The wheels are made of plastic, with ball bearings on either side to give a smooth fast ride.

Deck
The deck is made from 7 layers of wood, glued and pressed and finished with quality graphics.

Boarding Basics

Are you goofy?

This is how to find out. Slide across the kitchen floor in your socks: whichever foot leads your slide will be the leading foot on the board. If you slide with your right foot forward then you're goofy. If you slide with your left foot forward, then you're regular.

Moving off

This is how to move off. Put your leading foot at the front of the board over the truck bolts. Use your back foot as a paddle to push the board along. Once you're moving, put your back foot over the back bolts. Your feet should cover the bolts for your balance to be perfect. Bend your knees and spread your arms. You're off!

▽ grinding, street-style, on a customized board

A perfect air off the top of a ramp

Tic-tac, tic-tac

The tic-tac will keep you moving once you've pushed off. Lift the front wheels slightly off the ground and move the board to the left and to the right, pushing rhythmically with your front foot then your back foot. Soon you'll be moving forward like a sidewinder snake!

Can you Ollie?

There are loads of tricks and techniques to learn and quite a lot of new words – here are just a few of them!

Air	to turn around in the air at the top of the ramp
Fakie	turning the board round 180° to go backwards
Grind	to scrape along a surface on the trucks instead of the wheels
Carving	another word for turning the board
Ollie	a jump that is the basis for nearly all the skateboard tricks you can think of! When you jump, the board comes up with you.
50–50 Grind	ollie onto an object like a rail and grind both trucks along it
Boardslide	like a grind, but sliding along on the belly of the board instead of the trucks

Pride Comes Before a Fall

On his birthday Dan came downstairs wearing all his new gear: helmet, knee-pads, elbow- and wrist-guards, and hugging his new skateboard. It was perfect. He'd chosen all the parts himself, and assembled them with a bit of help from his dad. The graphics were just right. It was the coolest board – ever!

Dan took his skateboard outside. Down the side of the front path, separating it from next door, was a low concrete wall that was perfect for grinding. He'd never managed it with his old board, but that was a rubbish board. He'd fly like a bird on his sleek new one.

He began his run-up, but just then Slick Nick appeared, speeding up next door's path to his house. At once Nick stuck out his arm, blocking Dan's way, so Dan had to jump clear. Slick Nick was the best skateboarder on the estate, but he was always showing off, racing up behind the younger boys and messing up their moves, and jumping the queue at the ramp.

Slick Nick ollied up his front step and landed with a satisfying thud.

"Hi," he said, stepping off his board, "hear you're having a party at the skate park?"

"What if I am?" said Dan.

"You forgot to ask me," Slick Nick said.

"You're not asked," Dan said. "It's just for a few friends."

"Sure you don't want a class skater to show you some *real* moves?" sneered Slick Nick. He reached out and flicked Dan's helmet. "Only wimps wear all this gear," he said. "And anyway, you can't stop me going to the skate park."

Dan shrugged and picked up his board. "Keep out of my way this time."

"OK," said Nick, but as Dan walked back to start another run-up, he heard Nick's taunting voice shout "See you at the park, wimp."

But Slick Nick didn't turn up at the party, and everyone had a great time. Dan's new board carried him up the halfpipe like a rocket. He achieved an air-turn, at last, after months of trying. "My first air," he thought, glowing with delight. "That's made my day!"

"Sweet party, Dan," said his friends as they went home.

When Dan got back to his street, he saw Nick getting out of his dad's car. His face was badly grazed, and one of his arms was in plaster. His dad was shaking his head. "It's all your own fault, Nick. How often have we told you to wear your helmet and pads. Now you won't be skating for at least a month."

"Bad luck," said Dan as he skated past.

"Yeah. Guess I'll have to dust off my safety gear," said Nick, wryly.

Welcome to Alton Towers

MAGIC AND FUN FOR THE VERY YOUNG

Cred Street featuring Tweenies™

Tweenies™ Attractions
Tweenies™ Playground .... under 1.5m
Tweenies™ Theatre

Vintage Car Ride 1.0m*
Cred Street Carousel 1.3m*
Toyland Tours .... 1.0m*†
Frog Hopper 1.0m*

All rides state the minimum height allowed on a ride.
*Minimum height unless accompanied by an adult.
†Maximum 1.4m unless accompanied by a child.

Adventure Land

The Beastie 1.2m*
Gallopers Carousel 1.3m*
A selection of magical new play equipment designed to excite the imagination. Operating restrictions apply.
Squirrel Nutty's Ride .... 1.1m*†

Old MacDonald's Farmyard

New Ribena Berry Bish Bash .... 0.9m*†
Riverbank Eye Spy 1.0m*
Doodle Doo Derby 1.0m*
Old MacDonald's Tractor Ride 1.1m*
Old MacDonald's Singing Barn

Skyride – children under 4 must be accompanied

LAUGHS AND FRIG

Merrie England

Log Flume .... 0.9m min, 0.9m-1.1m*
Tea Cup Ride ...... 0.9m min, 0.9m-1.1m*
Swan Boats 1.3m*
New 3-D Cinema (shows from 11.00am every 20 minutes until ride close)

Gloomy Wood

New Duel – The Haunted House
Strikes Back! 1.1m*

Ug Land

Corkscrew 1.2m
UG Bugs . min. height 1.0m max. height 1.5m
UG Swinger 1.2m
Bone Shaker 1.2m

FOR FUN LOVERS

Katanga Canyon
Congo River Rapids . 0.9m min, 0.9m-1.1m*
Runaway Mine Train 0.9m min, 0.9m-1.1m*

The Towers
Hex® – The Legend of the Towers
. . . . .0.9m min, 0.9m-1.2m*

Towers Street
Towers Trading Co, Guest Services

Webmaster Adventure On Ice
A futuristic cyberspace adventure on ice. This show contains scenes that may frighten younger children. Check at the venue entrance or Guest Services for show times.

HIGH ADRENALIN RIDES FOR THRILL SEEKERS

X-Sector
Oblivion® 1.4m
Black Hole 1.2m
Submission 1.2m
Enterprise . . . . 0.9m min, 0.9m,-1.4m*

Forbidden Valley
Ripsaw 1.4m
Nemesis® 1.4m
The Blade . . . . 0.9m min, 0.9m-1.1m*
Air – sponsored by Cadbury Heroes . . . 1.4m
Dynamo 1.4m

Fastrack
On all standard and peak days, look out for our free Fastrack service on Air and Nemesis. Two queues will be operating for these popular attractions, either choose to queue normally or scan your park ticket at the Fastrack ticket dispensers (near the ride entrance) to receive a Fastrack ticket with a time slot. Simply return to the ride at any time during the period shown, enter through the Fastrack entrance and wait just a short while for your ride. This service is subject to availability. Rides and dates on which Fastrack operate may change. Further details are available on request.

Alton Towers –
all you need to know!

Distances to Alton Towers

	Miles	Km
London	161 m	258 km
Birmingham	46 m	74 km
Manchester	47 m	75 km
Glasgow	255 m	408 km
Bristol	141 m	226 km
Portsmouth	204 m	326 km

Disabled parking is free. For all other visitors travelling by car, there is a £3 charge per car, or you can opt for a premium parking space close to the entrance, at £6 per car.

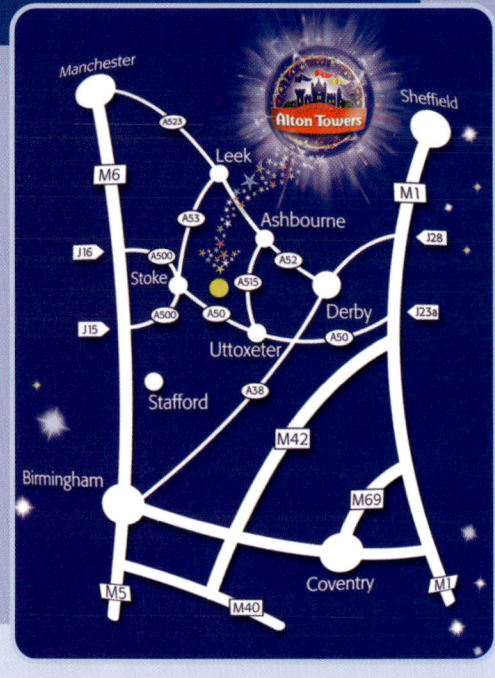

Opening Times and Prices

The Theme Park season is from April to November, with special events at different times, including a firework display and laser show at the end of the season around Hallowe'en. Grounds and gardens open at 9.30, attractions open at 10 and close at 5 (later in the summer). Prices start at £16.50 (for under 12s) and £19.50 aged 12 and over. The £66 family ticket covers two adults and two children aged 11 and under. There are special discounts for parties larger than 10.

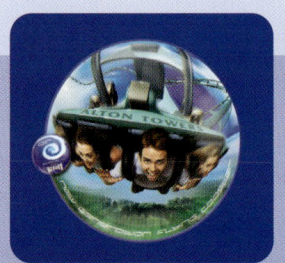

MAKE THE MOST OF YOUR DAY

STOP!
First things first, remember it's a day! Not a couple of hours or a few minutes. You have an entire day to enjoy the multitude of magical entertainment ahead of you.

So with that in mind:
1. Take time to read the gate map and plan what you want to do.
2. Review queue times as you enter the park. They are displayed on a screen at the bottom of Towers Street and elsewhere around the park.
3. Avoid leaving bags on ride platforms. It's easier and more secure to use the lockers at Guest Services.

FOOD
Don't forget to take a little time out from all the excitement to sit down to boost your energy levels. But bear in mind that lunch times in our cafes and restaurants can be pretty busy, so try not to visit them between the peak hours of 12 midday and 2 p.m.

SHOPPING
Rather than carry your shopping or ride photographs around with you, ask for them to be sent directly to the Towers Trading Co. on Towers Street. That way you can collect it all when you leave the park.

MEMORIES
Look out for the Fujifilm Photo Trail around the park to make sure you get the best spots for taking back great memories of your day out at Alton Towers.

GUEST SERVICES
If you require any information during your visit, or have any cause for concern, our Guest Services team will be happy to help. You'll find them in Towers Street, X-Sector and the Forbidden Valley.

CAR PARKING TOKEN
Don't forget to purchase your car parking token from selected areas in the park.

About Elephants

Elephants are mammals. They are the largest land animals in the world. The second largest is the hippopotamus, but a big hippo is only half the weight of a big elephant.

AFRICAN ELEPHANT

Appearance

The most distinctive feature of an elephant is its trunk. The elephant uses it to breathe and smell, as well as to pick up food and water. An elephant can suck up 55 litres of water at a time through its trunk.

African and Asian elephants are not quite the same. African elephants are larger than Asian elephants and they have bigger ears. African elephants' ears are fan shaped and can be as big as 1.5 metres. Asian elephants have smaller ears, triangular in shape. Their trunks are different, too. The Asian elephant has just one lip at the end of its trunk. The African elephant has two. The Asian elephant has two great bulges on its forehead. The African elephant's forehead is rounded without bulges.

AFRICAN

ASIAN

Both kinds of elephant have tusks. These are really over-grown front teeth. They are made of ivory. In Africa, both the males and females have tusks, although the female's tusks are shorter. In Asia, however, it is only the male who has tusks. The elephants use their tusks as tools and in feeding. Males also use their tusks to fight, usually over females.

ASIAN ELEPHANT

12

Habitat
Elephants live in herds on the African plains and in the jungles of south-east Asia.

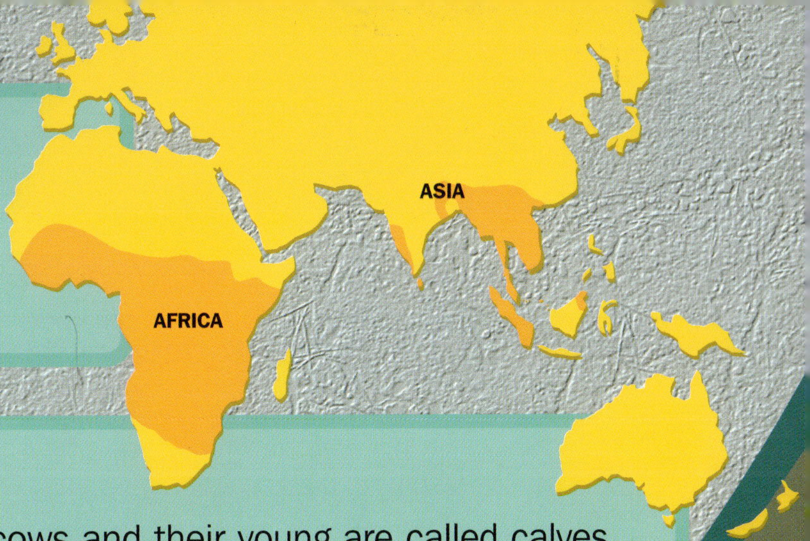

Breeding
Female elephants are called cows and their young are called calves. An elephant cow has one calf every few years. The cows and calves live in family groups, led by an old female called a matriarch. Male elephants are called bulls. Once they are 14, they go away to live on their own. Elephants can live for over 80 years.

Food
Elephants are herbivores. They feed on grass, leaves, flowers, fruit and seeds. They need to eat about 150 kg of food each day.

Endangered species
Elephants have no natural enemies except man. People do not eat elephants. They just kill them for the ivory in their tusks, which they make into ornaments. As a result, these magnificent beasts are in danger of dying out altogether.

ELEPHANT COW AND CALF

Key Facts about Hippos

large mammals

mainly found in East and Central Africa

live in lakes and rivers

spend up to 16 hours a day in water

hippos have special skin designed for life in water

have barrel-shaped bodies and stumpy legs

their large heads have ears, eyes and nostrils on the top, to keep them out of the water

Hippo walking on river bed

14

Hippos wallowing in mud

- can submerge for up to 5 minutes
- can close ears and nostrils and walk along the river bed
- toes are webbed
- leave the water at night to feed on grass
- herbivores

- have enormous jaws and huge teeth
- live in groups of 10–15
- are about 1.5 metres tall
- they can weigh up to 3,200 kg
- can be up to 4 metres long
- name means 'river horse'

Mighty Mammals

Hippopotamuses

'Hippopotamus' means 'river horse'. Hippos do spend much of their time resting in water, but they are more closely related to cattle than horses.

A hippo has good sight, hearing and sense of smell. Its eyes and nostrils are high up on its head, so it can stay hidden just under water and continue to see and breathe. It closes its nostrils and ears when completely under water. Hippos have glands in their skin which produce droplets of red liquid. This protects the skin from becoming too dry.

Hippos live in groups of females and their young. The babies are well cared for. They sometimes ride on their mothers' backs, perhaps to protect them from crocodiles in the water. The males must compete for territory and females. Hippos leave the water every night to feed. They eat mainly grass, but sometimes raid crops, causing immense damage.

Distribution
Rivers and lakes in East Africa and West Africa

Size
Head and body length up to 4.6m; shoulder height up to 1.5m
Pygmy hippo: head and body length up to 1.8m; shoulder height 0.75m

Weight
Up to 4,500kg; pygmy hippo up to 270kg

Number of young 1

Lifespan
Over 40 years in game park, in captivity over 54 years

Class Mammalia

Family Hippopotamidae

Number of species 2

Encyclopedia entry

Babies are well cared for

Creature Feature
Big Talkers

Earth's largest land animals have a lot to say – even when they don't seem to be making a sound.

Elephants make plenty of sounds that humans can hear, such as barks, snorts, roars and trumpet-like calls. But scientists have discovered that elephants also have a 'secret' language for communicating over long distances. This special talk is based on infrasound – sounds so low that humans can't hear them. The sounds can travel several miles, so the world's biggest land animals can keep in touch across grasslands and forests in Africa and Asia.

`Magazine entry`

WELCOME TO COLCHESTER ZOO!

Kingdom of the Wild is one of Colchester Zoo's latest developments, and is a most impressive exhibit. It is a multi-species complex, which houses a range of different African species ranging from Giraffes to Monitor Lizards and Spurred Tortoises.

The Pygmy Hippo

Kingdom of the Wild is also home to our Pygmy Hippos, Freddy and Venus. They are fed daily on various fruits and vegetables. Pygmy Hippos are rainforest-dwelling animals and are usually found near rivers or swamps. They are much smaller than their cousin the African Hippopotamus. The Pygmy Hippo spends little time in the water, unlike the amphibious ways of its larger relative.

`Guide Book entry`

Snakes

Reptiles
- over 3,000 species
- can be as small as a worm (13cm) or as large as a python (10m)
- cold-blooded, need sun to warm them before they can be active

Habitat
- found in all warm parts of the world, including seas and rivers
- some live in burrows, others live in trees

Appearance
- scaly, smooth skin – sheds when outgrown
- some have hinged jaws to swallow large prey
- no external ear – detects sound through the ground
- poor eyesight, cannot close eyes, transparent lower eyelid

Killing prey

- cobra kills by poison, injected through fangs
- python kills by squeezing – then swallows prey whole
- only one in ten is harmful to humans

Breeding

- female snake lays eggs, up to 100 in a clutch
- eggs left to incubate alone
- eggs soft but tough – not brittle like hens' eggs

Food

- all snakes are carnivores
- small snakes eat insects and birds
- larger snakes eat mice and small mammals
- very large snakes eat mammals as big as deer

Crocodiles

Where will I find crocodiles?

Do crocodiles smile?
Crocodiles don't smile but they look as though they are smiling. They have a gap in the side of their snout where the pointed fourth tooth sticks up. Even when the crocodile closes its jaws the tooth can be seen. If a crocodile loses a tooth it grows another. Its sharp teeth are excellent at ripping into its prey but as it has no molars it cannot chew food. It tugs and tears at a carcass and swallows it in chunks.

Big fellas
Take two big steps forward. You have just measured the length of the smallest adult crocodile. (1.5m)

Now take another 8 big steps. That's how long the largest male crocodiles grow. (6m)

Tough as old boots
Tough leathery skin protects the crocodile from predators. (No animal can bite through the crocodile's skin.)

blunt snout

webbed feet

powerful tail

Snip Snap!

The crocodile is a powerful swimmer but it is surprisingly speedy on land too. It can use its strong claws to climb up slippery riverbanks. The zebra who has wandered down to the river for a drink gets no warning as the crocodile darts forward and grabs it by the muzzle. The crocodile pulls its prey under water until it drowns. Then it wedges it under a ledge to stop it floating to the surface and eats it at its leisure.

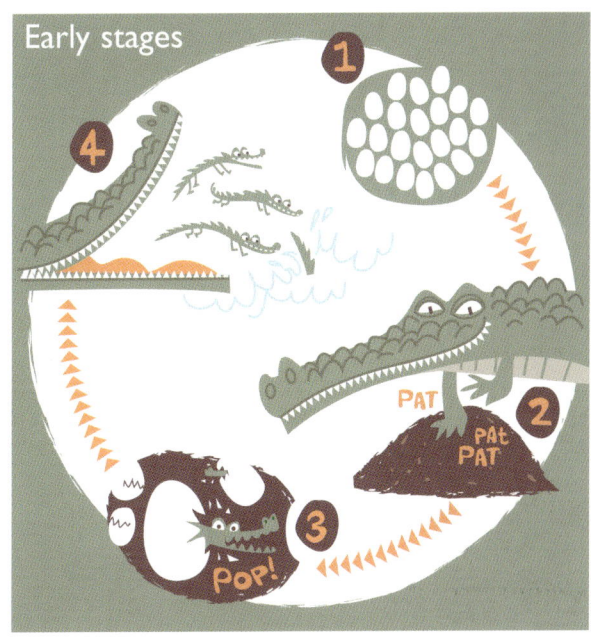

Sleepy head

Crocodiles often look as if they are yawning. They sit for hours with their jaws wide open. This is to help them reduce their body temperature. Crocodiles, like all reptiles, are cold-blooded and rely on the warmth of the sun to heat their blood before they can become active. If the crocodile gets too hot it just opens its mouth to cool down.

— short legs

Eggstraordinary!

The female lays her eggs in a nest in a sandbank and guards them until they hatch about 3 months later. When she hears her babies calling, she digs up the nest and carries the hatchlings in her mouth to the water.

Amazing facts

Crocodiles can close their nostrils and they have ear flaps which keep out the water. They also have a third eyelid which they can close to enable them to see when they are under water.

What's for dinner?

Crocodiles eat lots – frogs, birds, small mammals and fish and, of course, the odd human.

How to Make a Twizzer

What you need

Materials
- Template
- Thin cardboard (20cm x 8cm)
- Good quality string (70cm)

Equipment
- Scissors
- Large nail
- Glue
- Coloured pens
- Pencil

How to make

1 Cut out a disc from the template.
2 Place the disc on the cardboard.
3 Make two circles by drawing around the outside of the disc twice.
4 Cut out the circles. You now have two cardboard discs.
5 Glue the disks together.
6 Mark the holes from the template using a pencil.
7 Colour each side of the disc with a bold pattern.
8 With adult help, use the nail to make two holes.
9 Thread the string through one hole and back through the other hole.
10 Tie a neat knot in the loose ends of the string.

What to do

1. Pull the disc along the string until it is in the middle.
2. Put the fingers of one hand through one loop, and the fingers of the other hand through the other loop. Keep the knot out of the way.
3. Holding one hand steady, circle the other hand round and round, twisting the string as you do so.
4. When the string is twisted tightly, pull your hands firmly apart. This will make the string unwind and wind up again, causing the disc to spin.

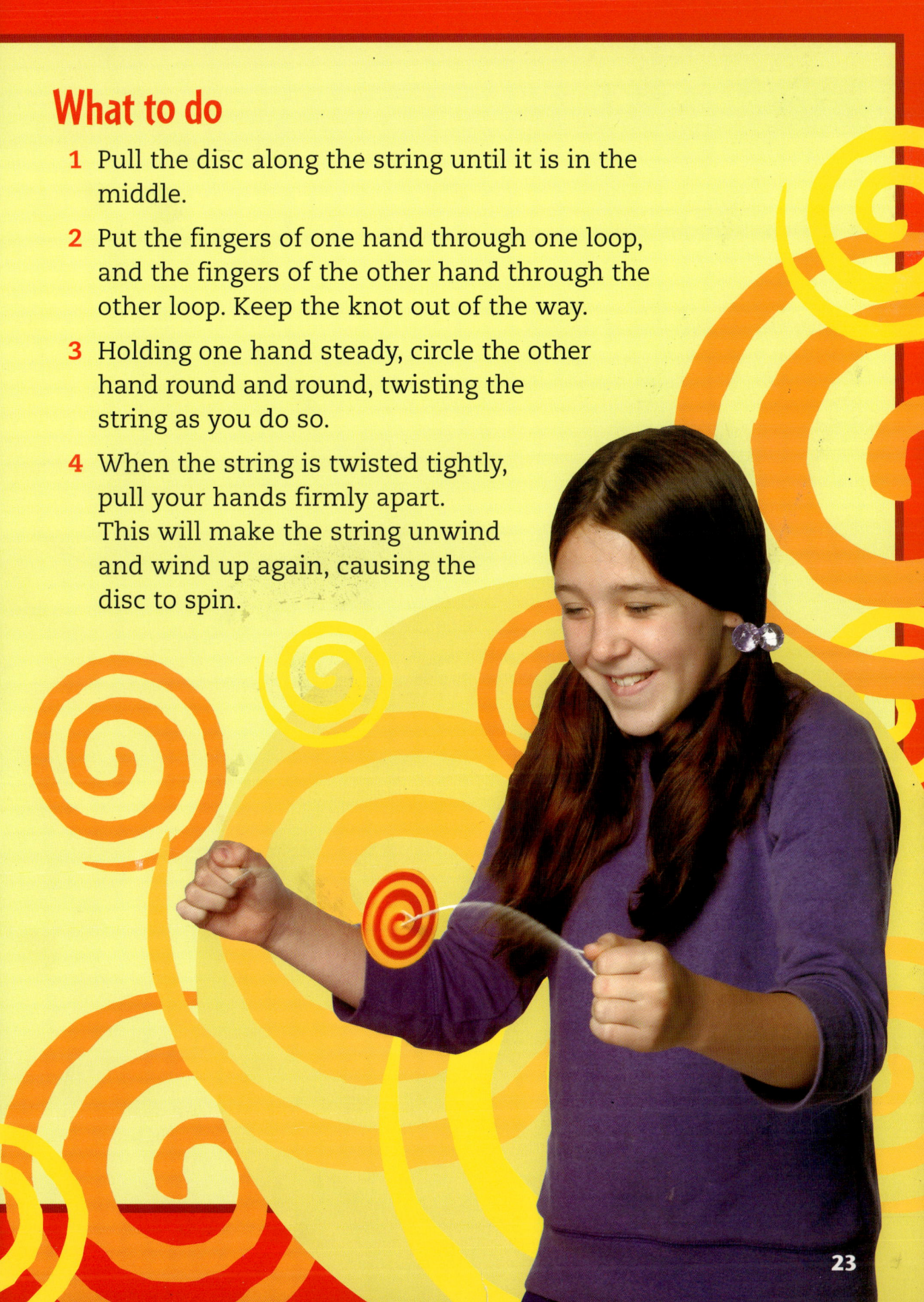

How to Make a Balancing Bird

What you need

- Scissors
- 2 x 1p coins or 2 x 2p coins
- Card (30cm x 30cm)
- Pencil
- Coloured pens
- Sellotape

How to make

- Cut out the template of the bird.
- Then draw around the outline shape onto the card.
- Very carefully cut out the shape.
- Next draw on the features (e.g. feathers, beak, eyes) and colour the wings.
- Finally tape a coin to the back of each wing.

  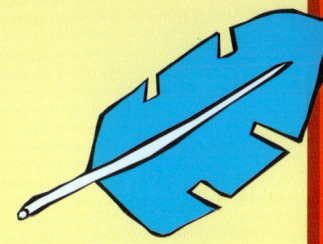

What to do

Place your bird on your finger. Balance it carefully and watch it wobble, but stay upright. Where else can you balance your bird – on top of a pencil? Anywhere else?

How to Play Tiddly-winks

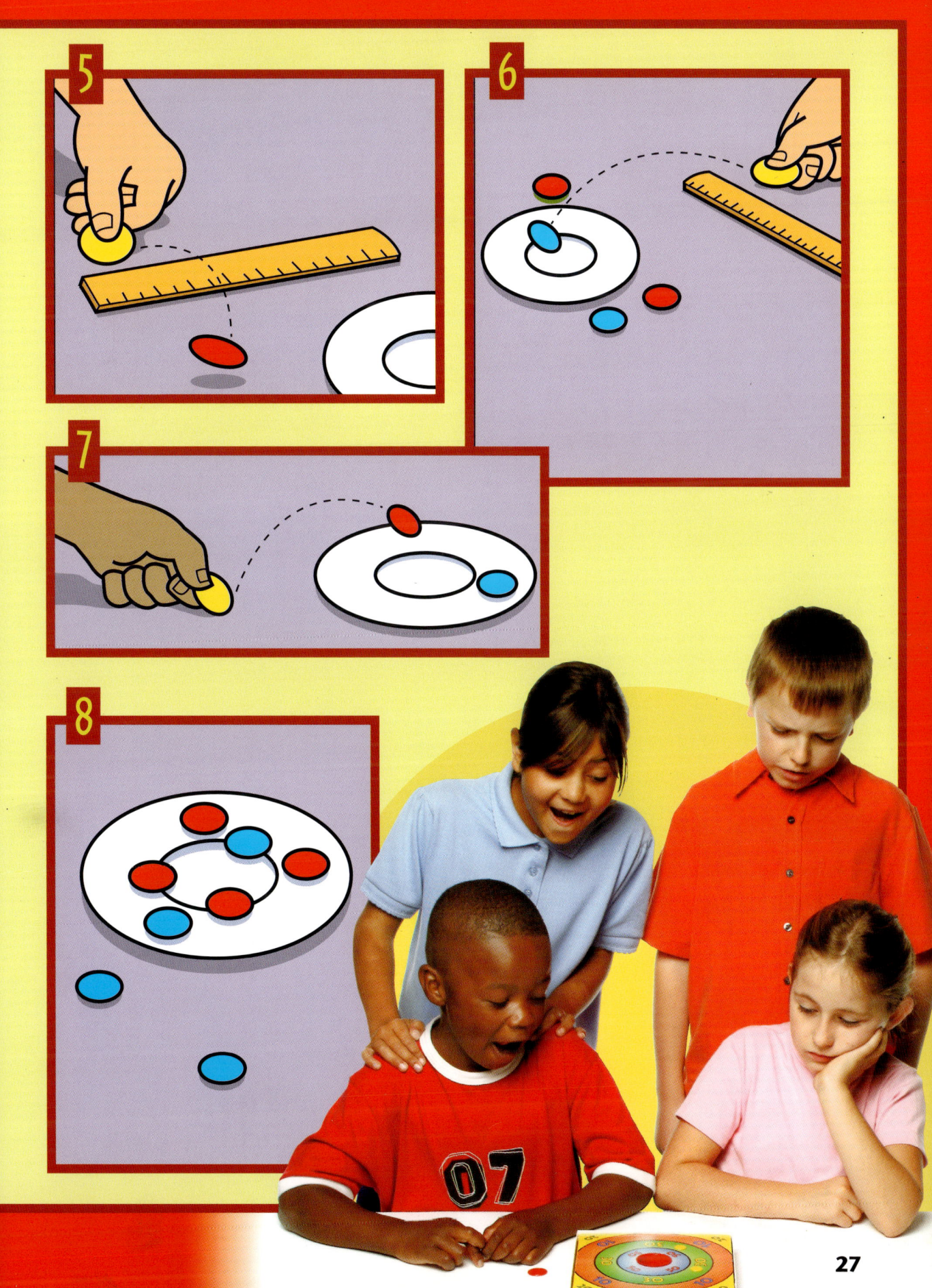

The Romans

Beginnings

There was a small tribe in southern Italy called the Latins. Around 800 BC they founded the city of Rome and started to call themselves Romans.

The Roman Empire

The Romans were a tribe of fighters and traders, and for the next thousand years they fought and traded from their base in Rome until they ruled all the lands around the Mediterranean Sea.

The Romans believed their gods wanted Rome to be the capital of the world. This meant they had to make war on the countries around. The Romans built up a huge army. It was well paid and well run. Even men from countries that had been conquered wanted to fight in it.

Hannibal was a general from Carthage in North Africa who invaded Italy. He led thirty five thousand men and thirty-seven elephants across the snowy Alps to attack Rome in 218BC. Ten thousand men and thirty-six elephants died along the way. Although he had many victories against the Romans, Hannibal never managed to conquer Rome itself.

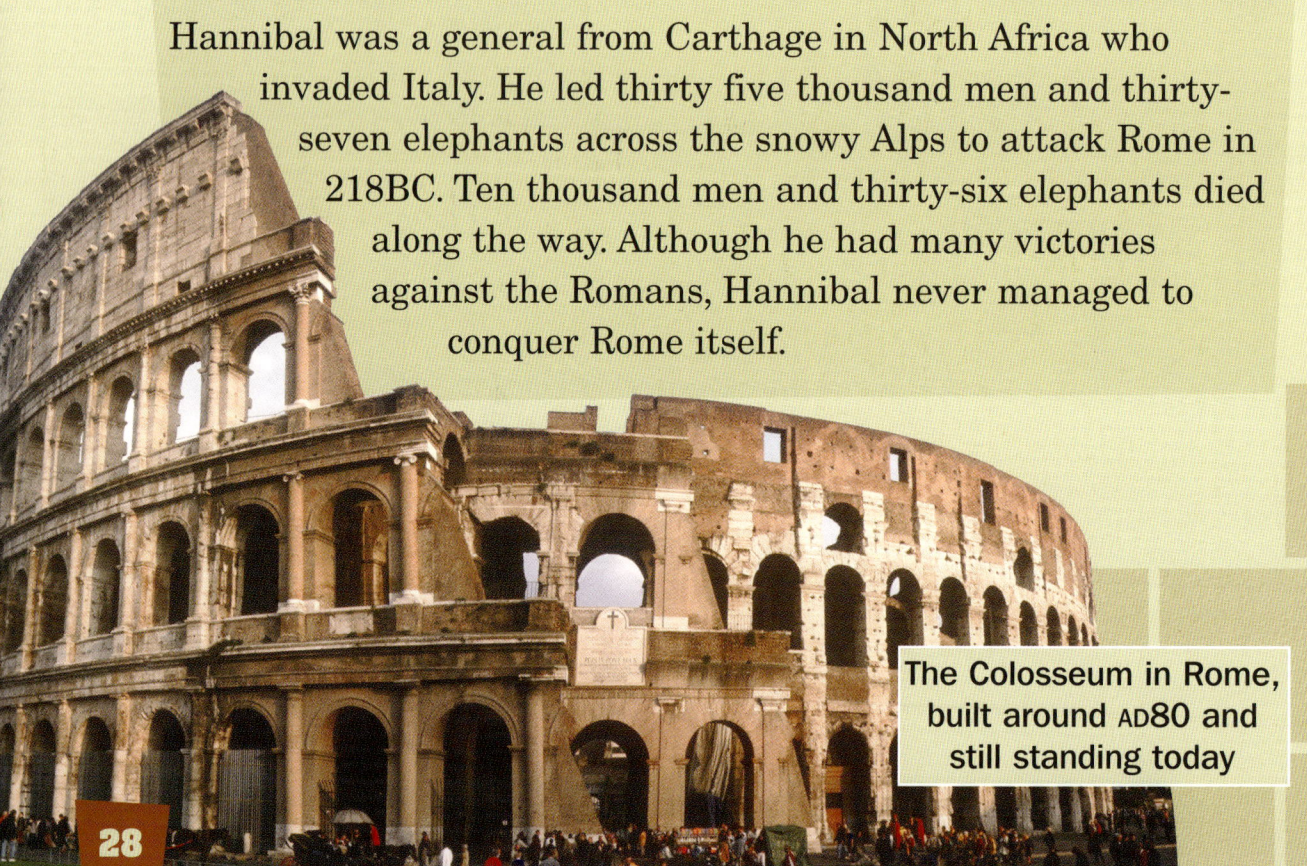

The Colosseum in Rome, built around AD80 and still standing today

Ancient carvings show how Romans lived.

The Romans in Britain

Over time, the Romans spread their control right across Europe and almost as far north as Scotland. By 128AD Emperor Hadrian decided the empire was big enough – it was getting hard to control. The Romans stopped conquering new lands. They built walls at the furthest borders and settled down to rule. Hadrian's Wall, in the north of England, was one of these walls, and it is still there today.

Life under Roman rule

Under Roman rule life was very good for some people and much less good for others. Wealthy Romans had slaves who were forced to do any jobs their masters gave them. While the well-off might eat seven-course banquets, most people ate much more simply – just bread and vegetables.

The Roman legacy

From one small city in Italy grew a great and famous Empire. Even today the influence of the Romans can be seen all over Europe – in roads, viaducts and buildings.

Map of the Roman Empire

Roman Sports and Games

Roman baths

Romans who were well-off had lots of spare time to enjoy their favourite pastimes. Men would visit the baths daily to bathe in hot and cold baths, exercise, meet friends, and gossip. Women went too, but at different times.

Fights at the Colosseum

The Colosseum opened in Rome in 80AD, and was the biggest arena in the empire. The crowd was mostly men; women were allowed to go, but they had to sit high up.
The games were bloodthirsty spectacles. Wild animals were brought from all over the empire. Bears, lions, crocodiles, elephants and wolves would be sent into the arena to tear each other to pieces. Gladiators would fight wild animals, or each other. Sometimes the Colosseum would be flooded, and ships would fight sea battles.

Gladiator fighting a leopard

Friendly games

Groups of friends played ball-games, and some enjoyed athletic sports that are still popular today, such as running, weights and throwing the discus. Another favourite way of spending time was playing board games that were like modern chess or draughts.

Public games

The Romans are also famous for great public games. Politicians paid for races, gladiator fights, and plays to make themselves popular with the people.

A Day at the Races

A huge crowd – more than a quarter of a million people – stream into the Circus Maximus (the name means 'great circle'). Everyone's looking forward to a great day out. The track is 600m long, and the chariots have to race round seven laps. The day starts when the chariots, pulled by two or four horses, parade into the ring.

The crowd wear the colours of their favourite teams. Rome's four teams are the Reds, the Blues, the Greens and the Whites. Lots of money changes hands as fans bet on their own team to win. A trumpet blows, a white flag is waved and – they're off!

Chariot on a coin

The races are exciting, and very dangerous. Drivers may be killed when their chariots crash as they go round the sharp bend at each end of the track. Charioteers who win get a purse of gold, and are famous stars.

By the end of the day the crowd has seen 24 races, with clowns, acrobats and fire-eaters coming on in the intervals.

GLADIATORS

Watching gladiator fights was a favourite Roman spectacle for nearly 700 years ('gladiator' means 'swordsman'). In 65BC the emperor, Julius Caesar, put on a show where 600 gladiators fought each other to the death in a single day.

WHO WERE THE GLADIATORS?

Gladiators were criminals, captured enemy soldiers, or slaves; a few were free men who earned their living fighting. A gladiator was trained to fight at a gladiator school by an ex-fighter (a *lanista*), and he could choose the weapons and armour that suited him best.

WHY DID GLADIATORS FIGHT?

Gladiators who showed skill and courage were the Roman superstars of their day. They fought just two or three times a year, and if they could survive five years, they could retire and live off their prize money. A slave or criminal could win his freedom.

DIFFERENT KINDS OF GLADIATORS

There were four kinds of gladiator. Three of them were called 'chasers' (*secutors*) because they wore armour and their fighting tactic was to attack their opponent with brute force.

■ Samnite – he wore heavy armour from head to toe: a large metal helmet with a visor, and metal or leather guards on his legs and sword-arm. He carried a sword or axe, and a large rectangular shield.

■ Thracian – he wore a bronze helmet (with a visor or a wide brim), and carried a curved dagger. He wore leg-guards, and carried a small round shield.

■ Murmillo – he wore a helmet and visor sometimes crowned with a metal fish. he carried a short sword and a large shield.

The fourth kind was a lightly-armed gladiator called a

■ Retiarius – he carried a net to throw over his opponent, a three-pronged trident or a dagger, and had just a shoulder-guard for protection. He could move fast, because he had no heavy armour. His fighting tactic was to use his skill, speed and cunning.

At the start of the games, the gladiators marched into the arena and saluted the Emperor, with the words "We who are about to die, salute you." At the end of each fight, the loser would hold up one finger, to ask for mercy. If the crowd felt he had fought bravely and deserved to live, they gave a 'thumbs up' sign. 'Thumbs down' meant the losing gladiator would be killed.

Children in Roman Times

Babies

Roman babies were given a name and a lucky charm (a bulla) when they were about a week old. Before then, babies that were sickly might have been left outside to die, and girls might have been given away. The father decided whether to keep the baby or not – the baby's mother had no say. If Roman parents got divorced, the children stayed with their father.

Children of slaves

If a baby's parents were slaves, the baby could be sold. If the child stayed in the master's house, it had to work as it grew up. Girls would help with cleaning, fetching water and washing clothes. Boys would help with working in the fields.

Slave girl helps her mistress

School

A few boys went to primary school at the age of six. They learned to read, do arithmetic, and to write on a wax tablet with a pointed metal pen (stylus). They left primary school aged 12. This was the age when girls were prepared for marriage, boys started work with their fathers, in their shop, workshop or on the farm.

Children's games

Life wasn't all school or work – Roman children liked to play too. They played with leather balls, and toys like the ones we still have today: hoops, marbles, board games, dolls and wooden animals.

What Roman children wore

Girls and boys wore short tunics with a belt around the waist. When they were old enough to marry, girls wore a long dress called a stola. Older boys wore a toga over their tunics. This was a long, half circle of cloth that was wrapped around their body.

Different lives

Children of important and wealthy families had a teacher at home. At 12, their sons started to study history, geography, and maths.

When a boy like this reached 14, his family held a special ceremony to show that he had become an adult. He took off the bulla from round his neck and put on new a white garment called a toga virilis. At 16 he learned how to speak in public, ready for a place in public life.

When a girl reached 14 or 15 she got married. Her husband would be older. She would have been taught how to spin and weave cloth, to manage slaves and run the house. Some girls also learned to dance, and play music, so that they would be able to entertain the guests at dinner parties.

Boy in a toga virilis

Recount

Winton Primary School
Winton
Westshire
PL4 3LS

1st June 2004

Dear Alice,

You wanted me to let you know how our Year 3 outing to Uplands Farm went. Well, the whole day was a great success.

We travelled to the farm by coach. The journey took less than an hour and, thankfully, none of the children was sick!

We were met at the farm by Mr Giles and his wife who couldn't have been more friendly. They told us the timetable for the day and we started off in the calving shed. The children were allowed to hand-feed two calves with milk from a bucket.

We had all brought packed lunches and we were able to eat them in an open barn where we sat on hay bales.

In the afternoon we had a tour of the farm, riding in a trailer on the back of the tractor. Mr Giles was very helpful pointing out all the features of the farm and answering the children's questions. (Jason asked how the hens laid their eggs in boxes!!)

Now for some practical advice: It is well worth insisting that the children all have wellingtons to wear, as it is muddy under foot. They will need their anoraks as well, as a lot of time is spent out in the open.

The children really enjoyed themselves. They have written some wonderful recounts of their day and we have already booked another visit for next May.

With best wishes,

Hannah

Hannah (Wright)

> Letter from a teacher to a teacher in another school telling her about the success of the Y3 outing

Complaint

Subject: Let the Ramblers Roam

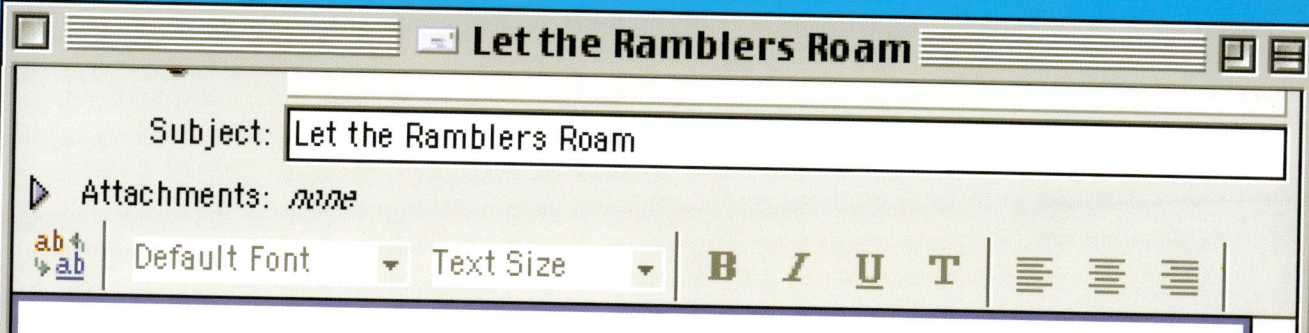

Sir,

I read with mounting anger your article 'Let the Ramblers Roam' (August 23rd), about how farmers stop ramblers from enjoying their walks by locking gates and blocking stiles.

I am a local farmer and four footpaths cross my land. I am happy to see responsible ramblers on my land but I know, from bitter experience, that not all those who wear hiking boots and carry rucksacks are responsible people.

Only last month, ramblers on my land left a gate open and my herd of cows got out. It took several hours to get them all back into the field.

Then, last week, a walker let his dog off the lead. The dog chased my flock of sheep and terrified them. The man tried to call off his dog but by then the damage was done. Two sheep later died from shock.

Up until now I have never locked a gate or blocked a stile but I am seriously thinking of doing so in the future.

Fred Giles
Uplands Farm
Westshire

E-mail from farmer to newspaper

Explanation

WESTSHIRE – A HAVEN OF PEACE AND TRANQUILITY

Mr F. Giles
Uplands Farm
Little Wetherby
Westshire
PL18 2NN

Tourist Information Bureau
County Hall
Westshire
PL1 7RE
Tel: 01777 452111
Fax: 01777 452112

3/4/04

My ref: DM/Best Kept Farm Competition

The Wealth of Westshire 'Farm Holidays' Competition

Dear Mr Giles,

I am writing to inform you that once again Westshire is holding a 'Farm Holidays' Competition. You are invited to take part in this important event which will encourage more people to visit our beautiful county.

The farm and its accommodation will be judged as follows:

- The appearance of the farm (tidy farmyard, machines stored safely, etc)
- The friendliness of the reception
- The tidiness of the rooms
- The quality of the furnishings
- The range of facilities (en suite bathrooms, microwaves, washing machines, etc)
- The range of activities (farm trails, feeding the animals, etc)
- Indoor facilities e.g. table tennis
- Standard of the garden (lawns and flower beds neatly kept, picnic area, barbecue, etc)

If you wish to take part in the Competition, please complete the attached form and send it to the above address. Inspectors will visit your property to judge it. Be prepared for this inspection any time after 1st May, as we will arrive unannounced.

Good luck, and may the best kept farm win!!

Yours sincerely,

D. Matthews

Debbie Matthews

Letter explaining the rules of the Best Kept Farm Competition

Congratulation

WESTSHIRE – A HAVEN OF PEACE AND TRANQUILITY

Mr F. Giles
Uplands Farm
Little Wetherby
Westshire
PL18 2NN

Tourist Information Bureau
County Hall
Westshire
PL1 7RE
Tel: 01777 452111
Fax: 01777 452112

My ref: DM/Best Kept Farm Competition

30/6/04

The Wealth of Westshire 'Farm Holidays' Competition

Dear Mr Giles,

I am writing to congratulate Uplands Farm on winning our 'Wealth of Westshire Farm Holidays Competition'. This is an outstanding achievement as there was stiff competition this year. You may be interested to know that 60 farms which offer Farm Holidays entered the competition this year and we awarded prizes to the following three farms:

Bronze Award: Greengates Farm, Lee Common
Silver Award: Hillside Farm, Oldford
Gold Award: Uplands Farm, Little Wetherby

As the winner of our competition you are entitled to put the 'Gold Award' seal on all your correspondence. We will supply a sign saying 'Winner of the Wealth of Westshire Farm Holidays Competition' which you can attach to your farm sign. We will feature all winners in our brochure about Farm Holidays in Westshire and I am sure that holiday-makers will flock to your farm and cottages this summer.

May I take this opportunity to congratulate you once again? All the judges commented on the attractiveness of your farmyard and the effort you had put into making your guests, in particular your younger guests, welcome.

Keep up the good work!!

Yours sincerely,

D. Matthews

Debbie Matthews

Letter telling Farmer Giles he's won the competition

Brochure for Uplands Farm

Come to Uplands Farm for the farm holiday of a lifetime

A warm welcome awaits you at Uplands Farm. Nestling on the edge of Brownley Moor and with spectacular views of the hills, this working dairy and arable farm will be your home from home.

We are situated on 200 acres of unspoilt farmland yet are only 7 miles from the M5.

Let us look after you

Accommodation is available in the 16th Century thatched Farmhouse where we offer two luxurious family rooms. We serve delicious farmhouse evening meals from our own reared meat and fresh vegetables from our garden. Our breakfasts will set you up for a day's sight-seeing in the beautiful countryside which surrounds our farm.

After your day out, come home to relax in our comfortable lounge with its inglenook fireplace and exposed beams.

Self-catering

If you prefer to be self-catered, why not stay in our award winning converted barn? Two luxury apartments have been created from the original stone barn, fitted with every comfort for your holiday. Each apartment sleeps 6 (a cot is available on request) and has a lounge, dining room and fully-fitted kitchen. There is a secluded garden with garden furniture and a barbecue.

Something for the children

At Uplands Farm we welcome children. So if your youngsters like feeding chickens, collecting eggs, caring for young calves or patting a friendly Shetland pony then spend your holiday with us. If they find the larger animals a bit scary, they can make friends with our two lazy cats and their adorable kittens or play with our young dogs, who like nothing better than being thrown a stick once in a while. Bring your wellies and you're welcome to help the farmer with all the jobs on the farm.

There's something for everyone down on Uplands Farm!

**WINNER OF THE WESTSHIRE
BEST KEPT FARM COMPETITION 2004
GOLD AWARD**

All Kinds of Letters

Dear Parents,
We are holding a meeting on Wednesday 2nd November at 7.30 p.m. about the 'Walk to School' project. As you know from the newsletter, we are keen to set up this initiative at King Street Primary.

Dear Mary,
Just a quick note to say thank you for the lovely lunch last Saturday.

Dear Mr Patel,
We are pleased to inform you that...

Dear Sir or Madam,
I wish to draw your attention to the appalling state of the pavement outside my house...

Please help us to continue our successful work,
Yours faithfully,
Dr. Stephen Brown

If I can be of any further assistance please let me know.

Yours sincerely,
Robert Turner

Do write back when you get a moment,

Love from

Jenny

See you at the match,
Cheers,
Matt

Play the 'letter' game

Choose a character from the left column to send a letter to someone in the right column. Is it a formal or informal letter? What are they writing about?

Gran	Megan (aged 9)
Mr. Kemp, Headteacher	Police officer
Ben (aged 9)	Solicitor
Mr Stephens, Plumber	Mr Dave Martin, Director of 'Save the Tiger'

Hobbies

Judo

Judo is a Japanese martial art, based on fighting without weapons. *Judoka* (people who do judo) learn particular holds such as the *Body Drop* and the *Stomach Throw* to throw their opponent. They wear loose trousers and a tunic, with different coloured belts to show what grade they are. Judo is taught at classes in clubs or sports centres.

Keeping lizards

Lizards make fascinating pets but need special care; ask an expert – a vet, a specialist shop, or a book. Lizards are cold-blooded so they need a heated home (such as a glass tank), with sand or gravel on the floor, and a rock or log to hide under or bask on. Some lizards eat insects, others plants, and they need clean water every day.

Magic tricks

The magician's art needs quick hands, a good memory and lots of practice. Tricks can be bought from a magic shop, or found in books. Simple props can be made or found at home. The magician's main skills are being able to: *palm* (hide something in your hand); *load* (hide things before the trick and then 'discover' them); or *ditch* (secretly get rid of something without the audience noticing).

Painting

Water-based paints are easy to use, and come in small blocks (to use with water and brush), or ready-mixed in pots (just use a brush). Paper comes in sheets or as a long roll, like wallpaper. Paint is put on with brushes, or even fingers. Simple patterns can be made by using a potato cut in half, with a pattern cut into the flat surface.

Snowboarding

Snowboarding can be done in the mountains, or on a dry slope. It was invented in the USA in the 1960s by keen surfers and skateboarders. Equipment can be hired or bought, and includes:
- The board – a *freeride* board is best for beginners
- Boots and bindings to strap and lock your feet in place
- A leash to keep the board attached to your leg
- Warm clothing
- Goggles to protect your eyes against snow glare.

Basic skills include learning to step, scoot and turn.

Yoga

Yoga is the art of relaxing by controlling breathing and movement. Yoga comes from India, and a few simple yoga stretching exercises practised every day make your body strong and help you feel relaxed. Different Yoga positions have names such as *Proud Warrior*, *The Lotus* and *Salutation to the Sun*.

SEA FISHING

Fishing from a beach can produce an exciting range of catches, as long as you're well prepared.

TACKLE

You'll need:
- **a long line** – at least 100m
- **a beachcaster rod** to cast long distances off shore
- **a rod rest** for when you change the bait
- **weights** – different sizes for different water conditions
- **hooks** – different styles for different kinds of fish
- **a fixed-spool reel** – easier for a beginner to use
- **a landing net**

COLLECT YOUR OWN BAIT

You can buy fresh fish and cut it up for bait. It can be more fun to collect your own bait, such as crabs, prawns, lugworm or ragworm.

WHEN TO FISH

Summer is a good time to begin shore fishing when fish come in closer to the shore to feed. High tide is the best time to catch fish; low tide is the best time to collect bait.

SAFETY MATTERS

Plan your trip carefully: find out what the weather may be like. Read the tide tables to know when high and low tides are, and make sure you fish in a place where a rising tide cannot cut you off. Wear suitable clothing: you can get wet and cold standing by the sea!

SEAMOUNT JUNIOR FISHING CLUB

Sea fishing is a hobby for people aged 7-77 years!

A great way to improve your catch and to make friends is to join a fishing club. Seamount Junior Fishing Club meets every weekend at the Old Harbour Boathouse. Boys and girls aged 7 and upwards are welcome to join. Family membership is available.

ARE YOU A BEGINNER?

The club offers lessons with an experienced angler. Bring your own tackle, or hire tackle from the club at reasonable rates.

BEEN SEA FISHING BEFORE?

Then try something new with the club – members can fish from the beach, off the harbour pier or along the river estuary. Fishing trips on the club's own boats can also be arranged.

Nick Mason, age 11, with his winning catch, a 10-pound cod.

'I caught this huge fish the first time I fished with the Seamount Club,' said Nick.

Membership is £10.00 per year for each child.

Safety First: members must be able to swim 50 metres.

Index

Alton Towers	8–11
balancing bird	24
chariot racing	31
Colchester Zoo	17
crocodiles	19
elephants	12–13, 17
African	12
Asian	12
gladiators	30
Hannibal	28
hippos	14–15, 16, 17
hobbies	44
judo	44
keeping lizards	44
magic tricks	44
painting	45
Romans	28–35
in Britain	29
children	34
Empire	28
legacy	29
sea fishing	46–7
Seamount Junior Fishing Club	47
skateboarding	2–7
snakes	18
snowboarding	45
tiddly-winks	26
twizzer	21
Uplands Farm	36–41
yoga	45